I0542666

THE SILENCE SOUND MAKES

and Other Poems

Nina Sokol

SPUYTEN DUYVIL

NEW YORK   PARIS

© 2023 Nina Sokol
ISBN 978-1-959556-22-0
Cover image: t thilleman, *Primordial Mirror*,
                        pastel on paper, 2020

Library of Congress Cataloging-in-Publication Data

Names: Sokol, Nina, author.
Title: The silence sound makes : and other poems / Nina Sokol.
Other titles: Silence sound makes (Compilation)
Description: New York : Spuyten Duyvil, [2023]
Identifiers: LCCN 2022060144 | ISBN 9781959556220
(paperback)
Subjects: LCGFT: Poetry.
Classification: LCC PS3619.O397 S55 2023 | DDC 811/.6--dc23/
eng/20221219
LC record available at https://lccn.loc.gov/2022060144

CONTENTS

IT IS
a house
of a
different
color. Across
the street
from where
I live
there is
a playground. The
house is
not in
that end. Furthermore,
it
doesn't
have a
shade. The
bed upon which
they are lying
is not in

it, either. The
last time
they spoke
to one
another the
sun had
been about
to set. She does
not remember
the words he
said. The
words that
could be
used
to describe
the bed
have
also van-
ished. If
I look out my

window I can
see the building
that is opposite
to where
the playground
is, but
not them. And
the bed
has been
moved to
a house
in the
other end
of the
solar system.

THE SILENCE SOUND MAKES
the space words
arrange pauses. Silence
was not a word
in the world,
once. No word was,
then, when
silence had no
need for sound and
no thought of
the world had
ever entered
it. The thought
of the world
was a word that
never left
it.

THE VASE

There had been
a sound in the
room that she
woke up in. The
vase had been
shattered and she
couldn't remember
whether the sound
had been a
word. She couldn't
remember the sound
to shatter, either. A
shadow rolled over
on its side
to stare at
her. The shattered
vase was reflected
in its eyes, like scattered

letters. On the
windowsill in the
painting above the
shadow was where
the vase had
stood, she remembered. She
tried to reach
out and touch the
meaning of it but
it was still wet
with paint. She
accidentally smudged
its outline into
the background
of the incoming
sky through the
window. And then
she opened her
eyes to the
word of
it.

ONCE THE
thought of
the world
entered
it
entered
into a
word.
Will what
was meant
before it
was said
ever be
heard?

THE CANDLELIGHT
flickers spark
reaches of
outer-space and
spans beyond. Some-
where
the sun
never sets or rises
and the sky
melts in-
to the land
auto-
matically. But on
earth there
are words
that
separate
things. He
parted her
legs in

the morning, poured
milk into
the coffee
and watched
it whirl
like stars
until he
thought he
heard the
word bang
at the
start of
eternity.

NOTHING BEGAN
the
world. There
was no bang
in a
universe. Silence
entered reluctantly.
By a
river on Mars
we sat and
stared into the
galaxy. And we
were listening
for a
star. We were
the deep
space emptying.
From
then on

silence
was only
a word.

SILENT SPACE
makes
spoken words
breaks and
shifts. Once the
word silence
didn't exist
it
was heard.
Nothing
was not
yet
known in
the world
because nothing
is the
sound of
a word. No-
thing, even
silence, always
is.

WORDS MAKE
lines and
faces
eyes and lips and
lakes and
skies separate in
the landscapes of
paintings, in
silence faces
fade into heads
and necks and
bodies slam
back in-
to them.

A LAKE LINES
a landscape like
the stream of a
poem heard
in a painting. But
beyond the edge
of the canvas
the paint of
the line trickles
to where the
word world begins.
Until then the
words line of
a lake remain in-
visible in a painting
like the line
of a poem
remains silent in

it. Even the
word painting
doesn't exist
inside of it.

EVERY WORD
has a syllable
in it
that wants
to blast the
sky through
its emphasis. Every
sky has
been punctured
by a star
from the
inside to
penetrate the
word of
it. A sky
consists of
random mor-
phemes
and scattered
particles of

light. Reach
out and try
to touch
its dispersal
with the
hand of
an earthling. Be-
yond
earth's
atmosphere
the sky
has never
been heard. Neither
has earth.

WHEN I
woke up
this
morning I
saw nothing
but in
the interior
of your
eye
earth
rise. Except
you were
not you
but the
shadow in
my life. There
are things
in the
world that
cannot be

described. You
always lie
beside me
at night, projected
against the
wall like
the solar
eclipse that
you are, like
a sun
of darkness
surrounded
by light. And
it is my
shadow that
created you in
the opposite
end of the
galaxy, in
what was later

to be realized
as in-
explicable
silence.

THE CANDLE-
holder
on the
table
was not
empty. But
the lavender-
colored
flowers of
the vase
were missing. The
lit candle
spread its
shadow across
the table
as though
the shadow
was its
essence and
the essence

of the
shadow reached
beyond the edges
of
the table. As
though
beyond
the edges of the
table was
where the
essence of the
table
was.

THE LINE OF
the lantern
is in the
picture. The
picture is
in the
mind of
the man. He
shuts his
eyes to
touch the
line with
his hand
but the
line is
in a
letter, not
an image. A
letter that
is in a

word makes
the line
of the
lantern separate
from the
rest of
the world, not
the line
in a
picture. Finally,
he lowers
his hand
in his mind
and opens
his eyes
to the line
in the
letter of
the word
lantern.

NOTHING WAS LEFT.
When she unlocked her
bicycle the sea
drowned out the
sound of the horizon.
Nothing could be
seen except leaves
of roses lifting
like smoke toward
the end of
earth. There was
the sound of a singing
bird as though
there was a sky above
the water's surface. The song
of the bird was filled
with exuberant pauses. There
had once been a forest
in there
somewhere. Now there

was nothing
but the roots
of a maple tree
spreading across
the ground like
the serpent-hair of
an upside-down
Medusa. She watched
as earth tipped
away from the
star it
had once
belonged to. All
the animals of the
world held their breath. The
planet fell
in
silence.

IT WAS
when I
swallowed your
star that
I tasted
the sea-salt
of millions
of millenia
and heard
the dinosaurs
roar as
the light
of the
moon was
reflected in
their eyes
for the
first time
and the
words that

exploded in
my mouth
would never
be heard
again.

Not in Our Town
(A Post Card from Kiev, 2019)

The apartment that we
are staying
at is too big. But
the view from
the balcony is
compact with
things. Tables, chairs,
people. The waiters
rush back and forth, the
eternal glow of
fairy lights framing
them. I
am writing
poems about
Bonnard and
getting nowhere.
The cafe below the ground

is between this world
and the next. Who would
have known?
Between the opera house and
the President's Palace there
are pastel colored castles and
the intricately
carved faces of
lions and elephants
that seem to
peer straight
into
the life
of everyone, to
want to speak. This
is the world
they
wanted to
say to
the world then

but
as usual no
one was listening.
There is a park
where two
women
sell home-made
blinis from
a stand across
from the
art museum.
There is
a big
statue
of an
imposing
statesman.
You blew up
the children
in the park

in the name
of a notion
you had. You
had never
seen
the statue.
The blinis
were warm
and fresh
off the pan. The
lines there
were always
long.
The man
sitting on
a bench
is
smoking a
cigarette. His
dog is

at his
feet staring
up at
him. The
burnt
ashes sprinkle
down to
the ground, one
small
flame after
the next.
Back in
the apartment
that is too
big I have
found a small
annex off
the kitchen, a small
wooden
porch that leads

out to a cluster
of green
trees, a forest
even. We are
in the heart
of
the city.

AT NIGHT
she speaks to
more people
in her dreams
than she could
ever dream
of by day. The days
are long and
silent. By day
is meant the
time in which
a planet dips
toward its star
so that some
might call it sunrise. By silent
is meant everything
left unsaid in
beds before sunset
so that some might
call it silence. Within

herself she
knows that
she doesn't
know the word
for it,
only that
she is the
silence that
is meant.

HE TRIED TO
capture her
face with a
line the way
the shadow
did that contrasted
the light. There was
a piano behind
him that no
one was playing. There
was no writing desk
next to him
just an empty space. The
plant that was standing
in the corner
didn't have a
name. When he
looked at her he
couldn't see
where the line

went down straight
through her face, just
like he couldn't see
it in his own reflection. All
he could tell was
where the
flowers
began their
descent in
the
tapestry
behind him.

I AM THE POEM,
silent,
impenetrable, the
last failed attempt
at a good
line, the seductive
words that
sound beautiful
but that you
don't want
to hear. Read
through once and
then forgotten, thrown
away like a one-
night stand, it lands
right between
the eyes
of you before
falling: a crumpled
piece of paper

lying at
the bottom
of your
mind.

I DON'T KNOW
how to do
this. I don't
know where
to begin. I
am writing things
that weren't
intended. Words
that have no
meaning. What
is the word that
is meant
when it is
said. What is
the sound of
an intention, an
attempt to
get to
the bottom
of a

thing. What
is the
heart of
the word
that can't
be said. The
part that
was intended
and the
part that
the world
intends to
forget.

Time spans
pierce high
horizons in
ruins across
minds that
seek to see
the other
side of
them. If he
looks to-
ward the sky
he can see
something with-
in. The height
of the Byzantine
Empire in the
eleventh century
a.d. If only
he could
reach out

and touch
the buildings
the way they
were then. Now
it is too
late, there
are nothing
but ruins
inside of
him.

EVERYTHING
is strange
this
winter
morning. There
is a new sound
in the universe that
hasn't been
heard yet. The bird
outside your window
is singing
to himself
for you. Yet
yet there is no-
thing
like the reader
to wake up
to. Your words
will penetrate
you in

ways the
world never
could through
him. Afterward,
the
storms of
the universe
won't ever
sound the
same; they
will be
perceived
as minor
waves. No,
they will be
remembered as
silence running
below your
words as
they fall

into place
through the
galactical rise
of his eyes
and the
stellular sparks
off his voice
as he chants
them for
you to
himself when
you awake.

Post Card from Kiev II

When we arrive
everything is
so different. We
are surrounded by
nothing but
gigantic Soviet
style buildings. I stay
inside in
the big
empty
kitchen where
there are
endless wires
outside among
the deep
green
trees and
three gigantic refrigerators

filled with water
bottles next
to the sink
and write. There
is a single
light bulb
hanging from
the ceiling. I
try to take
a picture
of it but
the kitchen
won't fit
in the
image.
At night
we read
poems by
Eva Ribich
in Swedish

at an outdoor
cafe. It
is okay for
me to say
where I
come from
here if any-
one asks, not like
in Belgrade, we
agree. In
the big apartment
there are tiny
photograhs of
large dachas, perhaps,
captured within
a much too
tiny frame. The dachas
are surrounded by
an endless forest, and
a woman sits in

one of them, peering
out from a
candlelit window
to a
world far beyond
me, to the city square,
even. Next to
her is
the wooden
icon of an
unknown
saint in flaming
red and bright
yellow. I try
to touch
the saint
with my
finger, to feel the
flame, but I
can't.

There are
numerous locks
on the door, locks
that intercept
one another
like the
passages
of stars
at night and
I don't remember
where they
are supposed
to turn or
when. I
graze my
finger across
each lock, trying
to comprehend
each pattern
and the idea

behind it, how
it intricately
interweaves
into the next.
They each seem
to have a story
to tell that
I cannot comprehend. At
first, it seems
like I
can't get
out, but
finally I find
a way
to enter
the
city.

LINES BREAK SPACES
of silence with
such words that make
the outlines of
leaves speak. Like
plants leaves are
silent until they
are seen through
lips when
streams of words
gush forth
between
them creating
the shadows
in the world
that separate
things.

THE MIND SITS SUC-
cumbing to un-
inspired spaces, listens
to voices it could
never imitate, the
one voice never
listened to, buried
beneath gravel, quiet
in the center of
earth's gravitational
destiny: lips, mouth,
tongue, larynx,
esophagus
     in
  descent all
silent in the face of
     me.

THERE IS SOMEONE
wishing they
were sitting
next to you, that
they could be
a part of
your life right
now, just as
you wish
you were sitting
next to someone
apart from
the person
you are
currently
sitting next
to. You
wish they
were that

other person
whom you
would wish
was someone
else if
ever you
finally
got the
chance to
sit next
to him
or
her. And he
or she would
wish you
were some-
one else,
too. The person

they wish
you were
but which
will never
be you.

THE WORLD IS
a word and
the world is
not
a word.

ACROSS THE
silent
void
of
this
and
other
eons
the
single
utter-
ance
of
time,
the
sound
of
a
word,
is

heard
at
the
very
tip
of
it.

BEFORE THE
word sound
silence didn't
exist. Some
thought you
could keep
a secret
by keeping
silent and
when others
were silent
they weren't
speaking. But
silence wasn't
a word, the
universe was
not yet
eternal or
deep. As
soon as

he let
go of
her hand
in the
middle of
the night
it felt
as if
she was
floating. To
see the
world before
words became
sound changes
the sounds of
them. He
posed an
insignificant threat
to the
universe, fell

asleep and
dreamt that
he parted
her perfect
lips that
night and
broke through
silence before
there was
a word
for it.

WAS THE
world the
world before
it was
a word
he wondered.
He was
trying to
help her
remember so
that she
could tell
him. But
she couldn't
get herself
to explain
what she
had seen
with words.
She couldn't

comprehend it.
He poured
himself another
glass of
wine before
the sunset
and watched
the sun
make its
descent down
the crimson
landscape of
the bottle
in front
of him.
On some
planets it
is called
sunrise. He
lit a

final cigarette
and thought
about when
he came
between the
silence of
her perfect
lips last
night. It
wasn't the
sun that
was moving
it was
the planet
that was
turning.

THE WORLD

words make
spaces it
in design.
What he
heard when
she spoke
of herself
to him
wasn't a
language. He
knew that
he played
a minor
role in
her life.
Certain patterns
are ingrained
early before
there were

words to
create them.
The layers
of the
earth would
never have
been known
as layers
had it
not been
for words. The
order of geological
strata would
never have
existed, nor
would the
notion of
time.
She couldn't
explain why

there were
things greater
in her
life than
him. Sometimes
all she
seemed to
want was
to be
outside of
society, he
thought. To
speak in
the space
before words
were meant
and a
pattern was
made.

BLAST LANGUAGE
sounds beyond
reason to
understand them,
she said. He
didn't understand
what she
had said. He
comprehended
it. What
we had
was unique
yet unacceptable,
so society
had to condemn
it. Condemn
me. Imagine. Who
is me. Not this
no one before

there was
a language
since no one
didn't exist,
then. The vast
nothing. The
sheer bliss. That
must have
been me. And
I was free
then because
I wasn't
a sound
yet. Just
like silence
couldn't be.
Only later
was the I
I would be-

come condemned.
By society, you
mean?
That
too, yes.

LIKE THE
recurring
theme of
a silent movie,
the earth
is a word
in the
universe.

An Example of a Letter (of Response) to the Dawn of the Third Millenium

This is
what it
could
be:

Let me
slip your
mind open
for you.
Let me
make every
single splash
of blood-
red hue
behind

your closed
eyelids stream
out of
you, every
sparkling
drop, a
vomited
star falling
from a
nauseously deep
sky.

It could
also be
a reminder
of an
eruptive line
gladly given
to some
unassuming

biological thing,
the
memory you
have of
delivering
a message to
what you
thought was
a person
back when
humans still
wrote letters.
There was
the story
of the
human who
wanted to
see the
world remain
a part

of this
millenium
and of
the human
who
had obsessed
over another
too
hard in
its mind.

We non-
earthlings
are way
above any
of those
things.
Human:

there are
so many
corpses at
the bottom
of your
baffling skull
that you
couldn't tell
the difference
between
the intricate
calibrations of
a shattered
brain and
the sound
of your
own heart
breaking.
You wouldn't

be able
to hear
them.
All they
want is
to rhyme,
they
have a
song to
sing, too.

Let
me tell
you some-
thing
about
you that
will make
you cringe. The

world is
full of
species like
you and
always
has been. Did
you really
think you
were the
first of
your kind?

Soil-
worshipper, soul-
searcher, we
know you:
you sold
your soul
to the

forces
within, yet
the universe
loves you –
listen
to it
sing.

NINA SOKOL is a poet and translator in the midst of translating plays, poems and novels by Danish writers. She was a grant poet-in-residence at The Vermont Studio Center in 2011. She has received several grants from the Danish Art's Council to translate plays, including a play written by the fairy tale writer H.C. Andersen which was published by the journal *InTranslation*. She has also translated numerous novels by such writers as Robert Zola Christensen, Kristian Himmelstrup, whose novel, *Pio*, has just been nominated for next year's DR Roman Prisen (prestigious literary prize in Denmark), Thomas Lagermand Lundme, and Anna Grue (Danish crime novelist). Translations of poetry include Mikael Josephens' trilogy (excerpts of which also appeared in the journal *InTranslation*). Her own poems have appeared in American journals, including *Miller's*

Pond, the *Hiram Poetry Review* and the (Australian) *Verandah Journal* and a collection was published (*Escape and Other Poems*) by Lapwing Publications in Belfast, Ireland (2015).

The Silence Sound Makes is Nina Sokol's second poetry collection which probes the question, among others, is it possible to escape language and enter silence when language is the only means through which we can comprehend it?

www.ingramcontent.com/pod-product-compliance
Lightning Source LLC
Chambersburg PA
CBHW011224120626
46545CB00010B/3144